W9-AZZ-654

A GIFT FOR:

_____

FROM:

_____

DATE:

_____

OUR TRIP ACROSS AMERICA

BRUCE & STAN

Stories We Heard About

Courage

ON OUR TRIP ACROSS AMERICA

Bruce Bickel &
Stan Jantz

GIFT BOOKS
from Hallmark

BOK3051

COUNTRYMAN®

Contents

Behind Every Life
is a Story.

Introduction

We're two ordinary guys, but we had an extraordinary adventure. We spent the summer driving across the country. Now, that event isn't extraordinary in itself. In fact, many people have performed the feat. But most folks drive across country in an attempt to complete the task as quickly as possible. The memories of those trips are long hours on the inter-state, fast food wrappers scattered on the car floor, and no personal contact except with the cashiers at the old-fashioned gas stations (the ones that have pumps and don't accept credit cards) and the occasional tollbooth operator. (People who are in a real hurry, or particularly antisocial, save time and avoid contact with even the tollbooth operator by keeping lots of coins in the car and using the "exact change" lane.)

Our trip was different. It extended over three and one-half months, so speed was obviously not an issue. We drove over 10,000 miles (which proves we didn't take the short route). But the *duration* and *distance* were not what made our trip extraordinary. The most intriguing aspect of our trip was the *people* we met and the *stories* they shared with us about their lives.

The purpose of our trip was to interview people. We were doing the research for a book (*Bruce & Stan Search for the Meaning of Life*), so we spoke with everyone, everywhere (even tollbooth operators and gas station cashiers). We had meaningful conversations with over 1,000 people. (That figure *doesn't* include the people we passed on the street or sat next to on the subway or stood next to in the elevator, with whom we exchanged limited pleasantries. Actually, we didn't even exchange pleasantries with the people in the elevators. We didn't want to break the unwritten rule of elevator etiquette, which prohibits talking or making eye contact.)

We expected to learn a lot about the meaning of life by talking to people (and we did). We learned so much, it could fill a book (and it has). But the unexpected pleasure was learning about the personal stories of the people we met. We heard fascinating stories about people. Some of the stories involved tragic events; some were encouraging. All of them were life changing—for the people who actually lived the stories and for us as we heard them.

Our lives will not be the same because of the people we met and the stories we heard. If for no other reason, we have a greater appreciation for people because we learned this very important lesson: *Behind every life is a story!*

What makes these stories so amazing is that they involve regular people. We didn't talk to any celebrities.

Just plain folk. People like us . . . and you. (This assumes you aren't chauffeured around in a limo and don't live in a mansion. If you're like us, you're more concerned about paying the mortgage than avoiding the paparazzi. In fact, we're only interested in "paparazzi" if it's a new flavor of Ben & Jerry's ice cream.)

In this book we've included several of our favorite stories we heard while "on the road." They all have a common theme of courage. Most people (ourselves included) think they have courage until the time it's actually needed—then it's in short supply. The people in these stories, however, kept their fears to themselves and had enough courage to move ahead with their lives. They even had enough courage to share it with others. That's the interesting thing about courage. It doesn't eliminate fear; it gives you the ability to conquer it.

We suspect that you'll be inspired by these stories. We

were. Perhaps they'll motivate you to reflect on your personal stories and the lessons you can learn from your own life. Perhaps they'll make you more interested in the life stories of your friends and your neighbors. Perhaps they'll encourage you to be more interested in the people you don't know as well. Remember: *Behind every life is a story!*

Bruce & Stan

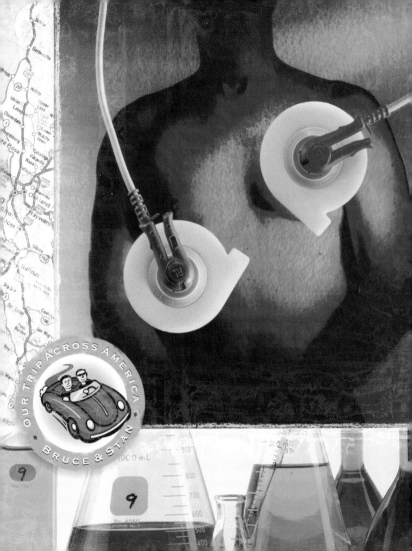

F

or Jim Westgate, 1999 was the year of dying.

You hear about people who survive an accident or a disease in a miraculous way, but you rarely hear about someone who experiences miracle after miracle in the process of traveling on a journey, as Jim puts it, "up to the doors of death and back." That's the kind of story we heard—a story so remarkable you can't help but wonder how one person could have such courage.

You have to begin by putting Jim's story of courage into context. At sixty-one years of age, Dr. Jim Westgate, who holds a doctorate in Urban Ministry, is a gifted teacher and leader. He has helped pioneer a national program known as "One by One." This program seeks to rebuild

The courageous conquer fear by transcending it.

—ANONYMOUS

communities one youth, one family, one block, and one neighborhood at a time. He has worked tirelessly to help the poor, and he teaches others at the graduate level to do the same. Jim and Nancy, his wife of thirty-seven years, enjoy a productive and fulfilling life.

Jim has always been an energetic, optimistic person. So when he began losing energy and weight, he knew something was wrong. At the beginning of 1999, his heart began to beat rapidly and irregularly. It was a warning sign he didn't take lightly. His grandfather, father, and uncle all died of heart complications, and his brother had recently received a heart transplant. The doctors discovered two blocked arteries in Jim's heart and did an angioplasty, but that didn't solve the problem. The irregular heartbeat continued and worsened, leading the doctors to implant a pacemaker.

Amazingly, these procedures had no effect. Jim continued to lose weight and got weaker and weaker. "I was sliding downhill," Jim said. "I realized my life was slipping away." The doctors tried to stabilize his worsening condition with medication, but on two occasions he nearly died from a toxic reaction. The second time Jim ended up in the hospital, where he and Nancy called out to God in frustration. "God, we can't get a handle on this," Jim prayed. "My life is sliding away." Yet even in the midst of their confusion and pain, Jim sensed God's power. It was a power he would call on again and again in the incredibly difficult months ahead.

My gracious favor is all you need. My power works best in your weakness (2 Cor. 12:9).

When the money runs out,

or your health is in jeopardy,

. . . you can turn to God

and He will be there.

No appointment is necessary.

KEEPING GOD IN THE SMALL STUFF

Jim went to see a heart specialist in Redwood City, California, and was diagnosed with fatal heart disease. His left ventricle, which was more like a sponge than a muscle, was literally blowing out. Jim needed a heart transplant immediately. Within days he was transferred to the Stanford University Medical Center, renowned for its expertise in heart transplant procedures. A battery of tests came to the same conclusion, only the situation was even more grave. Jim's heart had become so unstable he was asked to stay in the hospital until a heart became available. He was connected to a defibrillator, which would shock and restart his heart if it stopped beating. It was June 28, and the news was about to get a whole lot worse.

When they arrived at the hospital the doctor approached Jim and Nancy with crushing news, and it had nothing to do with his heart. In a CAT scan procedure, the doctors had discovered a mass on Jim's right kidney. Specialists in urology and radiology confidently said, "This is a classic pattern. We've seen thousands of these. It's cancerous, and we need to remove it immediately."

"We were absolutely shattered," Jim recalls. "What this meant was not just another operation. If I had cancer, then I could not go back on the heart transplant list for three to five years because the immune suppressant drugs they must give you make your heart a place where melanoma and lymphoma flourish. Two years earlier I had a malignant melanoma removed from my left arm, so I was already pushing the envelope."

The doctors suggested various ways to keep Jim's heart going for a period of years, but it was wishful thinking. Their real concern was the kidney operation itself. With Jim's heart in such a weak and critical condition, they weren't confident that he could "come out the other side."

"It didn't look good at all," said Jim. "You don't even

know how to pray. You talk about this all your life, but you don't know how to pray when it happens. We gathered as a family and actually planned my funeral. I don't know if you've every thought about doing that, but it's a pretty awesome experience. Then I wrote letters to my wife, my son, and my daughter. I wanted to tell them things so they could remember me. We prayed, and we knew people from all over the country were praying with us. Suddenly we sensed God's power all over again."

Jim instantly recognized three things about God's power and the courage it gives us. "Not only does God give us the power to face deterioration," he said. "He gives us the power to face the darkness. And then He gives us the power to face death."

Even when I walk through the dark valley of death, I will not be afraid, for you are close beside me (Psalm 23:4).

Jim woke up on July 5, the day of his kidney surgery,

needing a miracle. In his weakness, he needed God's power, and that's what He received—three times over. Jim refers to the events of the next three weeks as his "Three miracles."

Miracle Number One — In all likelihood the surgeons would have to remove the entire kidney in order to get the mass, reducing Jim's chances for a heart transplant to near zero (most people can live on one kidney, but two are necessary to handle the intense drug therapy required to survive a heart transplant). But they only had to take a portion of the kidney, and Jim came through the surgery just fine.

Miracle Number Two — Nearly one hundred percent of the time this type of mass on the kidney indicates cancer. That's what the doctors were expecting when the tissue was sent to pathology for analysis. During the seven days of waiting for the test results (can you imagine what that week was like?), Jim and Nancy continued to pray. Admittedly

God doesn't use illness to punish us.
God uses illness to teach us.

---

they struggled. They wanted the mass to be noncancerous, but they also knew the overwhelming odds against it. So they asked God to walk with them through the days of darkness "no matter what the circumstances might be."

When you go through deep waters and great trouble, I will be with you. When you go through rivers of difficulty, you will not drown! When you walk through the fire of oppression, you will not be burned up; the flames will not consume you. For I am the Lord, your God, the Holy One of Israel, your Savior (Isaiah 43:2–3).

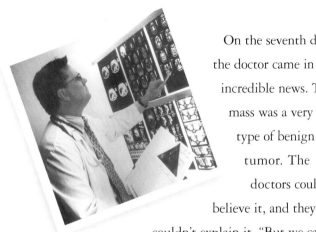

On the seventh day, the doctor came in with incredible news. The mass was a very rare type of benign tumor. The doctors couldn't believe it, and they couldn't explain it. "But we can," said Jim, "because we know Jesus has the power to do those kinds of things. And He has the power to sustain us when we have to look death in the face."

The doctors couldn't believe it, and they couldn't explain it.

Miracle Number Three – On July 26, just three weeks after his kidney surgery, Jim received news that a heart donor had been found. This was the biggest miracle of all, because people often wait months, if not years, for a suitable donor, and sometimes they die before getting a heart. Jim's donor was a young man killed in a motorcycle accident whose family wanted to donate his heart. Within hours Jim was on the operating table in Stanford University Medical Center receiving his new heart. "They took out my heart, put me on a pump for two hours, stuck in the new heart, put my chest back together, and that baby started to pump!" Jim said enthusiastically. "In just seven days—just seven days—I was out of the hospital after having a heart transplant! That's another miracle."

The Lord says, "I will rescue those who love me. I will protect those who trust in my name. When they call on me, I will answer; I will be with them in trouble. I will rescue them and honor them. I will satisfy them with a long life and give them my salvation" (Psalm 92:14–16).

While in recovery at Stanford, Jim became friends with a fifteen-year-old boy who had also received a heart transplant. The young man asked his doctors if he could see his old heart, and Jim decided to go through the experience with him. "It's really amazing," Jim told us. "They always save your old heart for research purposes, and if you ask, they'll show it to you. My new friend and I were wearing rubber gloves in this place called the gross lab, and they brought us our hearts. Mine was in a blue towel, and I got to hold it. I can't begin to describe the emotions and the sense of closure I felt. It was remarkable." (Jim also told us he had a sudden urge to toss the little fist-sized rascal across the room, then he laughed.)

Six months after his heart transplant—near the date of his sixty-first birthday—Jim went to Stanford for one of his weekly biopsies to see if his body was either rejecting or accepting his new heart. He had been doing well, but his body had been showing a slight amount of rejection. Not on this day. "The results came back and I had a zero!" Jim said, his face beaming. "That means my heart loves me and I love my heart. I love my heart, I tell you!"

You thrill me, Lord, with all you have done for me! I sing for joy because of what you have done. O Lord, what great miracles you do! (Psalm 92:4–5)

It's hard to keep a good man down, and that's especially true with Jim Westgate. He expects to be teaching again soon, and already he's been sharing his story publicly. Recently he spoke in his home church about the three ingredients—out of which came the three miracles—that gave him the courage to go through his year of dying.

"The first ingredient is the *power* of Christ to face deterioration, darkness, and death," Jim explained. "The second ingredient is the *people* of Christ, who came along-side Nancy and me and sustained us in the midst of all this. You see, the roller coaster is so terrifying, you need someone there to walk with you through these experiences. You need someone to talk to about your doubts and your questions. You need someone to stand with you when you get that devastating news, when the entire world seems to fall apart and darkness just sort of hangs around you. And you need someone to be able to share the miracles with you and rejoice with you because it brings transformation to you and to them as well."

Jim will always be grateful for the three miracles, but even more important than those is the third ingredient, and that's the *presence* of Christ. "We didn't always know the miracle was going to happen. God was gracious in giving us the miracles, but a lot of people don't experience the miracles. I want to tell you that we were ready. If the kidney had been cancerous, we knew Christ was going to be present with us. If I didn't survive the heart transplant, we knew Christ would be sufficient."

As we traveled, we heard stories about many different types of courage. When you hear a story like Jim's, however, you can come to only one conclusion. The courage that comes from God is the best courage of all, because it has nothing to do with you, and everything to do with Christ.

O Lord my God, I cried out to you for help, and you restored my health. You brought me up from the grave, O Lord. You kept me from falling into the pit of death! You have turned my mourning into joyful dancing. You have taken away my clothes of mourning and clothed me with joy, that I might sing praises to you and not be silent. O Lord my God, I will give you thanks forever! (Psalm 30:2–3, 11–12)

When people think of New York City, they generally think of Manhattan, home of all those famous New York landmarks like the Empire State Building, Times Square, and Broadway. When we traveled through New York, we stayed in Manhattan, but we didn't really see New York in all its variety.

New York is actually five counties, or boroughs. Manhattan was the first borough established, and it's the one visitors like us usually see, but it's not the largest or the most populated. Queens is the largest and Brooklyn is the most populated of New York's five boroughs, which also include the Bronx and Staten Island. The Bronx has a certain mystique (Yankee Stadium is in the Bronx), and your hear a lot about Queens (the Mets play their games at Shea Stadium in Queens), but there's something about Brooklyn that brings to mind that certain New York attitude (you know, the kind of attitude that says, "Hey, you talkin' to me?").

While we were in New York, we heard a story about a remarkable young woman who is making a difference in the lives of many people throughout this borough of over two million people. Her name is Barbara Williams, and she's a member of the New York Police Department, the nation's largest. That she's a member of the legendary NYPD and a woman isn't all that unusual; what makes Barbara unique is her title. Her business card reads: Rev./Det. Barbara Williams. Not only is Barbara a cop, she's an ordained Pentecostal minister as well. And she doesn't leave her preaching in church behind some pulpit. Barbara takes her Good News message right onto the streets.

If you're speaking words of truth, kindness, and encouragement, then your heart is in great spiritual shape.

KEEPING GOD IN THE SMALL STUFF

Her bosses on the force know her as "the officer with a badge and a Bible." In fact, they were the ones who noticed her gifts and gave her the title Reverend Detective. Because Barbara has such an ability to communicate with people on the street, the NYPD deputy commissioner of community affairs says she doesn't just bring a police presence into the community. "She brings the community into the police."

Barbara grew up in Brooklyn, so the streets are familiar to her. She was a cop before she became a minister, and for the first three years of her police career she walked her beat talking to anyone who would listen about what it means for the city and the church to work together. To this day she talks with young people, community activists, and fellow clergy.

The New York subway is always an experience.

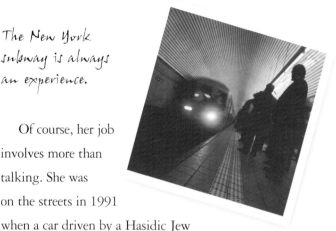

Of course, her job involves more than talking. She was on the streets in 1991 when a car driven by a Hasidic Jew accidentally killed a black child in Crown Heights, an area with a large population of orthodox Jews. Four days of rioting ensued, culminating in the retaliatory and fatal stabbing of a Hasidic student from Australia who was totally removed from the accident. It was a rough time, but Barbara kept her cool. In fact, her courage in the face of difficulties and her ability to handle the stress of her job have led to many opportunities to counsel fellow officers.

God doesn't see your circumstances as insurmountable. He's not intimidated or discouraged by them.

Barbara takes it all in stride. She didn't set a goal in her life to become either a cop or a minister. "I wanted to teach," she said, "and I had an interest in surgery. Blood and stuff doesn't scare me." She may not be a doctor, but Barbara's skill and courage in working with hurting people on a daily basis qualify her as a healer of sorts. "If you can change one person," she said, "that person will change another."

New York City the big melting pot.

The Great Hall at Ellis Island.

OUR TRIP ACROSS AMERICA
BRUCE & STAN

OUR TRIP ACROSS AMERICA

BRUCE & STAN

Courage at the Curb

Back in the days of Lewis and Clark, courage was a necessary component of any cross-country journey. There was danger lurking at every bend of the path. Sometimes there wasn't even a path. You needed courage just to put one foot in front of the other. Without it, you just froze in your tracks. (Of course, Lewis and Clark knew that if they refused to press on, they'd be nothing more than snow-covered statuary or stationary bear food. Maybe the courage to continue comes a little easier with those alternatives.)

Few people believe that courage is required if you're a tourist in America in the twenty-first century. Where's the danger? You pop your automatic transmission into "drive"

A terrifying goal doesn't
have to be dangerous . . .
but it should stretch you
so far that you wonder how
you will ever reach it.

KEEPING GOD IN THE SMALL STUFF

and you head down the interstate. Well, we've got news for you, Buckeroo. It takes a lot of courage to travel across the United States these days; at least, it took all that we had.

Courage is the character quality of moving beyond your fears. We had lots of opportunity to test our courage as we drove from the East Coast to the West on a circuitous route of over 10,000 miles. And no place tested the resolve of our courage more than the street corners in Manhattan where we tried to hail a taxicab.

Cab hailing is an art form in New York, and most tourists don't have a clue about the art. And they never will. It's indigenous to the Big Apple residents and work-force. The rest of us *schmucks* will never be able to imitate it. We suspect it has something to do with attitude, but we're not real sure.

Tourists in New York are doubly disadvantaged. Not only are they completely devoid of the requisite cab-hailing skills, but they lack the necessary street savvy for judging traffic flow. If you're a sightseeing rube in New York (as were we), the consequence of this double deficiency is that you'll be in jeopardy of either:

a) being run over by a cab as you step from the curb because it isn't stopping for you but is racing fifteen feet further up the block to pick up a real New Yorker, or

b) being elbowed to the ground by a New Yorker who has just rushed from a building and is intent on stealing the cab that stopped for you.

A significant portion of our first few days in New York was spent cowering on the curb, intimidated by both the Kamikaze cabbies and the combative New Yorker pedestrians. But we finally determined it was time to move beyond our fear and muster our courage at the curb. Intent on hailing the next cab and making it our own, Bruce leaped from the curb and stood in the street in front of the

There's even a memorial to dead cab-hailers.

on-coming traffic
with his hand out-
stretched. Like
Moses with his arm raised
to part the Red Sea, Bruce had managed
to bring the traffic to a halt, and we sauntered with a
New York-kind of attitude to the cab that was still rocking
from its sudden stop just inches from Bruce's femur.

When Bruce recounts this story, he elaborates about the
sensation of courage that welled within him and over-powered
his fear. When Stan tells the story, he confesses that he
pushed Bruce from the curb into the oncoming traffic.

Sometimes courage needs a little boost.

Incredible Courage

Our cross-country trip began on June first and concluded on September fifteenth. Most of that three and one-half months was spent in major metropolitan cities (Boston, New York, Chicago, Seattle, Los Angeles, etc.). But driving between the big cities took us through some quiet, rural country. That's certainly what we found in southern Oregon as we drove down Interstate 5 from Seattle to the San Francisco Bay Area.

Just outside of Medford, Oregon we stopped in the Applegate Valley. (Even the name sounds tranquil, doesn't it?) This is a quiet, sleepy region of our country, or so we thought as we arrived on a Saturday afternoon. It didn't stay so quiet the next day. As the sun rose on that Sunday

The meaning of "glory" is gift, literally a gift of honor and praise. In everything we do, God wants us to glorify Him.

morning and the rest of the nation stayed snuggled in bed, 8,000 people were scurrying about in Applegate and the outlying regions preparing to convene at the Applegate Christian Fellowship Church. That's right. The average Sunday attendance at Applegate Christian Fellowship is 8,000!

We couldn't image that there were 8,000 people in all of southern Oregon, so we felt compelled to investigate this phenomenon.

Applegate Christian Fellowship isn't like most churches.

The first thing you'll notice is that the sanctuary is an outdoor amphitheater that seats about 5,000. In beautifully landscaped surroundings, a hillside has been terraced with grass-covered tiers where people sit. At one end of this outdoor arena is a raised, flower-covered mound that is occupied by a band, which leads the worshipping crowds in praise choruses. (It takes two separate services in the outdoor arena to accommodate the crowds in the summer; in the winter, they move indoors and have five separate services.)

As spectacular as the setting might be, it's not the reason so many people attend Applegate Christian Fellowship. The real reason is the second thing you notice about the church: it's senior pastor, Jon Courson. Jon is difficult to miss. His stature and physique might remind you of WWF wrestlers (the fit ones, not the fat ones). And his red hair and beard only add to his eye-catching appeal. But 8,000 people don't

God is the only
unfailing place for your faith.
He always makes good on
His promises.

KEEPING GOD IN THE SMALL STUFF

attend Applegate Christian Fellowship to look at Pastor Jon. (We said he was big, but we didn't say he was handsome.) They go to hear him teach from the Word of God. Jon has a God-given gift of finding truth in the Bible and applying it to the everyday circumstances of life.

Pastor Jon doesn't give a sermon that sounds like he lives in an ivory tower on some isolated monastery far removed from real life. Jon knows all about the real life that the rest of us deal with on a daily basis. He can relate to the problems and heartaches of real people. And when he talks about the comfort and courage that God can provide in the midst of tragedy, he speaks from personal experience.

Back in the spring of 1982, Jon was taking a day off to go skiing with his wife, Terry. Someone from the church was staying with their three children: Peter (age 4), Jessie (age 2), and Christy (age 1). As Jon and Terry drove to Mt. Bachelor, their car hit some black ice, spun around, and slammed into a tree. Jon has no memory of any events after the crash until he was in an ambulance on the way to the hospital. He immediately asked about Terry. The paramedic said, "She's fine." "No," Jon said, "she's in heaven." They were both right. Terry was fine because she was in heaven.

Jon says that an amazing thing happened in that ambulance. He heard the voice of God. In what seemed to be an audible voice from heaven, Jon heard these words:

"I know the thoughts I think toward you,

Thoughts of peace and not of evil,

To bring you to a glorious end."

Upon hearing those words, Jon slipped back into unconsciousness until he reached the hospital.

As Jon was being treated in the hospital for his injuries, he received a phone call from his friend and

The person dependent on Christ has the amazing ability to maintain a steady ship on a stormy sea.

---

mentor, Chuck Smith, in Southern California. Chuck had received news of the crash and Terry's death. "Jon, I don't know what to say, except God has laid one verse on my heart that He wants me to share with you," Chuck said on his end of the phone. Then he quoted a verse from Jeremiah 29:11:

I know the thoughts I think toward you,

Thoughts of peace and not of evil,

To bring you to a glorious end.

What Jon had heard in the ambulance was an actual

Jon with his
daughter, Jessie.

verse he had never
discovered
before. Now it
was clear that God wanted
him to place that verse deep within his
heart. At the age of twenty-nine, Jon had suffered the tragic
death of his beloved Terry and had three young children to
raise. He needed courage to go on with life—the courage
that comes from knowing God has a plan for your life.

God blessed Jon's ministry in the years that followed.
As a single dad raising three little kids, Jon had lots of
material for sermon illustrations. The church family at
Applegate Christian Fellowship learned how God (the

heavenly Father) cares for us (His children) through Jon's analogies to his personal experiences with bath time, meal-time and potty training. Jon's struggles were very public. The only private matter he never shared with his church was the verse he heard in the ambulance and from Chuck Smith on the phone. The only other person who knew about the verse was Rick, an elder in Jon's church, who was with him in the hospital when Jon received the call from Chuck. For some reason, Jon wanted to keep the episode of the verse as a private, personal matter, and Rick respected Jon's request to keep the episode confidential. Neither of them ever told anyone about it.

God did have plans for Jon's life. Those plans included a new marriage several years later to Tammy, a beautiful woman (on both the outside and the inside). Tammy became the new mother to Peter, Jessie, and Christy. Those plans also included the subsequent births of children Mary and Ben. God's blessings on the Courson family were evident to everyone in the Applegate Valley.

It was clear that God's thoughts about Jon were good indeed. But God's good thoughts do not always mean that life will be without hardship and heartache. Jon had already experienced his share of that, but God's plans included further opportunity for Jon to experience God's hope and courage in difficult circumstances.

Jessie was a senior in high school when Jon was talking to her about boyfriends and how to find the right guy to marry. (Both of us have a daughter, and we have had similar discussions with them. It's Lecture #17 in the Father's Handbook.) Jon was explaining to Jessie that she needed to find a guy who could bring spiritual leadership to their marriage; she shouldn't settle for just any Christian guy;

not just a Christian guy who loved the Lord, but also one who had spiritual maturity. "Find a man who can lead you in spiritual truth," he told her. Jessie responded, "But where am I going to find a man like that? I won't be able to find such a man unless I go to a church where they have a good preacher." They both had a good laugh over that comment. (That's what makes Jon such a good dad and a good pastor. He can laugh at himself. And those who know Jon well say there is lots about him to laugh at.)

Before school the next day, Jessie stopped in at the church to participate in an early morning worship service. Jon was also there. So was Rick, who was leading the singing. As people took turns sharing and praying, Jessie stood and uttered a prayer that went something like this:

"Lord, I thank you for the promise in Your Word that says:

'I know the thoughts I think toward you,

Thoughts of peace and not of evil,

To bring you to a glorious end.'

Amen."

Jessie had quoted that verse without knowing the significance it held for her father. But Jon and Rick knew, and Rick composed a song on the spot using that verse for the lyrics. He sang it as the group concluded their time of worship. At the end, Jessie signaled her dad with the "thumbs up" sign from across the room, and she drove off to school.

It was only twenty minutes later that one of the other pastors from the church came to Jon with the message that a car wreck had been reported. The car was a yellow Volkswagen and the driver had been killed. While the identity of the driver had not yet been determined, everyone knew that Jessie drove a yellow Volkswagen.

Jon raced home. As soon as he saw Tammy, he knew that it was Jessie's car in the crash. Moments later, Jon's son,

Jessie, a true
reflection of
God's love.

Peter, walked into
the family room. He had
been one of the first people at the
scene of the accident. He blurted out, "Dad, she
found the Man. She found the Man." Peter was referring to
Jon's conversation with Jessie from the previous night. Yes,
Jessie was in heaven with Jesus Christ, and He was the Man
who could lead her into spiritual truth.

If your spouse had been killed in a car wreck, and if fifteen
years later your child was killed in a similar manner, you
might wonder if God really is in charge—if He really does

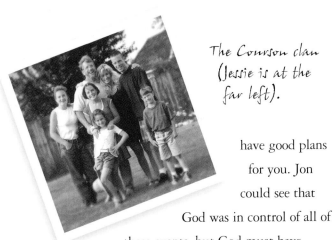

The Courson clan (Jessie is at the far left).

have good plans for you. Jon could see that God was in control of all of these events, but God must have known that even Jon's spiritual courage could use a boost. So, several months after Jessie's death, God made it clear that everything was going according to His plan.

Jon and Tammy had stopped at the post office to get their mail. (There's no home delivery where they live). Mixed in with their other mail was an envelope addressed to Jessie—in Jessie's own handwriting. Jon and Tammy stumbled over to the little bench outside the post office and held the unopened letter in their hands for a while as they wondered at the mystery. Then they remembered a tradition of their church youth group. (Every January, the kids at Applegate Christian Fellowship write letters to themselves in which they express their spiritual goals for the upcoming year. The following January, those letters are mailed, so the kids can be reminded of what the Lord has accomplished in their lives during the previous twelve months. It hadn't occurred to anyone that Jessie had written a letter to herself the January prior to her death. And nobody noticed her envelope in the sack with hundreds of other letters that were delivered to the post office several months after she died.)

Jessie and the other kids had been asked to answer this question: "If Jesus could do one thing for you this year, what would you want it to be?" Jon and Tammy opened the letter expecting to read a lengthy essay written by

Jessie. (Like her dad, Jessie couldn't stop talking when the topic was about Jesus.) To their surprise, and with tears in their eyes, they read the brief, five-word response that Jessie had written:

"To take me to heaven."

This was no plea of desperation from a despondent teenager. Jessie was a straight "A" student; the head cheerleader; the youth worship leader. She had a love for life that was exceeded only by her love for her Lord. Jon and Tammy were not saddened as they read Jessie's letter. They were encouraged. They remembered that it was written shortly after Jessie had attended a retreat where Jon had preached about the return of Jesus Christ. She was excited about the prospects of going to heaven and being face to face with Jesus. They were excited because they knew that's exactly where she was and what she was doing.

Just like He promised in Jeremiah 29:11, God had a

plan for Jessie, and it involved a glorious end—an end that brought her into God's presence in heaven.

That letter proved to Jon, once again, that God is in charge. The knowledge of that fact gives him the courage and confidence to stand on the flower-covered mound in the amphitheater at Applegate Christian Fellowship in front of thousands of people every Sunday. And despite the tragedies he's known in life, Jon can say from personal experience that God is faithful and true to His promise when He says: *I know the thoughts I think toward you, thoughts of peace and not of evil, to bring you to a glorious end.*

110
Downtown

OUR TRIP ACROSS AMERICA
BRUCE & STAN

Santa
Barbara Ventura
SANTA
Oxnard
LOS ANGELES
Long Beach
Pasadena
Anaheim
San
Bernardino
Riverside

Creative Courage

Hollywood is a difficult town. Of course, that depends on your perspective. If you're a struggling actor, director, or producer, Hollywood can chew you up and spit you out like yesterday's news. So many people come to Hollywood with dreams and plans for stardom, only to be crushed by the weight of reality. On the other hand, if you're just a couple of guys like us, who want nothing more than to meet a few people in the "industry" (that's what they call the film business here) and talk about the meaning of life, it can also be tough. It isn't that people aren't accessible. We found a number of directors, an aspiring actor, and a noted film score composer who were more than willing to talk with us.

Our challenge was getting around in Hollywood—as in going from one place to another. Even though the Los Angeles basin is known as the car capital of the world— there seems to be at least one vehicle per person here, and there are fifteen million people—it is certainly not the speed capital of the world. You're actually less likely to be involved in a fatal accident in Los Angeles than just about anywhere else (we're not making this up) because the average speed on the freeways is something like twenty-eight miles per hour. On the surface streets it's even slower. The bottom line is that trying to drive from any point A to any point B anywhere in Los Angeles is an arduous process.

The other thing that's difficult for the uninitiated is that all the places where actors and directors and producers work—namely the film and television studios—are heavily guarded. We don't mean there are fences with razor wire and uniformed guys with machine guns staring at you behind

Give your cares to God,

give your problems to God,

and most of all,

give your worries to God.

KEEPING GOD
IN THE SMALL STUFF

Fred in his office at Sony Pictures in Hollywood.

mirrored glasses. The Hollywood studios are much more subtle. They build these grand arches (just like you see in the movies) over every entrance, and right there in the middle of each arch is a little hut with at least one uniformed person and one of those flimsy retractable arms across the road that don't look capable of holding back a Geo Metro, let alone the substantial vehicles Hollywood executives and successful actors drive (read: Humvees, Expeditions, and Mercedes S500s, all in black, of course). But the balsa wood barrier does its job, because you wait patiently while "Carl" the studio guard checks to see if you're on the list of people approved to visit the studio that day.

We had an appointment at Sony Pictures with a Hollywood insider, and after twenty minutes he gave the go ahead to enter. His name was Fred, and he actually came down to meet us, which was very nice. Fred gave us a quick studio tour, and we even got to see the construction of a movie set and the filming of a television show. We tried to act casual, like we belonged there. This was very difficult (you can't help but be star struck, even if the stars are in their luxury trailers), especially when Pat Sajak walked by eating a soft ice cream cone. (Bruce wanted to yell out, "I'd like to buy a vowel," but Stan and Fred quickly restrained him.)

Fred took us to his office, a rather modest space for an Emmy winner and a much-in-demand film sound editor. He was in the middle of working on a major picture for

Sony, but he took the time to talk to us about the meaning of life. We recorded our conversation on our nifty Mini Digital Video camera, and we were about to leave when we noticed a large framed animated poster on Fred's wall. There were two very unusual things about the poster that caught our attention. First, it was an original color drawing, featuring several familiar Disney cartoon characters and a bunch of signatures at the bottom. Second, standing in the middle of the drawing was a lone human figure, and it looked just like Fred.

"What's the story behind this drawing," we asked.

"Oh, that," Fred replied. "I used to work for Disney, and some of the animators gave me that when I had leukemia for a year."

We stared at him blankly. "You had leukemia for a year? How did that happen?"

"Well, my white blood cells started multiplying, which

The Disney drawing.

led to a shortage of red blood cells, which led to infection, bleeding, and all kinds of fun stuff," Fred deadpanned. "Oh, and I almost died." (Fred has a very droll sense of humor.) "The Disney people gave me that drawing when I was finally able to leave the hospital. Of course I still couldn't work for almost a year. It was quite an experience, but I don't recommend it."

We were stunned. Here was this successful film editor who almost lost his life, and yet he was talking about his near-death experience as if it were nothing. We were wrong, of course. Fred was dead serious about the nature of his illness, and he was quite positive about the way he survived.

"The doctors told me, 'We'll do everything we can to savve your life, but it's God who's going to heal you,'" Fred told us. "So the only thing I could do was pray. But it's hard to pray when you're undergoing radiation and all those other delightful things they do to you when you have one of the big diseases. I prayed plenty, but it wasn't my prayers alone that did the trick. I had literally hundreds of people praying for me, and I could feel it. God gave me strength through the prayers of His people, and ultimately He

Bruce & Stan with Fred.

delivered me from death. The only explanation I have for it is prayer."

We left Fred's office and the Sony Pictures Studio lot terribly impressed. We had just conversed with a creative, crazy, compelling guy whose courage to overcome life's most difficult circumstance came from his incredible sense of humor and the very serious prayers of his friends. The two things—the humor and the prayer—seemed at opposite ends of the spectrum, but the more we thought about it, the more it made sense. The courage to fight against seemingly insurmountable odds doesn't always come from gritty determination and self-will. Sometimes it comes from resting completely—and not so seriously—in God's ability rather than ours. At least that's the lesson we learned from Fred's story.

OUR TRIP ACROSS AMERICA
BRUCE & STAN

PUBLIC
MARKET
CENTER

FARMERS MAR

SEATTLE

Courage to be Unique

You meet a lot of interesting people when you travel, especially in the cities. Invariably you see someone dressed in some kind of unusual costume, and he's holding a sign that says, "Will tap-dance for food," or he's just sitting there on the sidewalk looking strange, hoping you'll throw a quarter into his hat. These are the kind of characters most people avoid, although they can't help but stare from a safe distance (at least that's what we do).

In Boston, near Harvard Square, we saw a guy dressed up like an angel. He was standing perfectly still, with his arms stretched out like he was hovering or something. A guy in Times Square in New York was wearing what looked like a giant (and not very convincing) rabbit outfit.

Your lifestyle should
be in response to God's love,
not an attempt to
win His love.

KEEPING GOD
IN THE SMALL STUFF

In New Orleans we passed a "psychic" working from a lawn chair in front of his van (we knew he was a psychic because of the hand-written cardboard sign). Despite their best efforts, none of the colorful characters we saw along the way stirred anything in us except curiosity. None except for C. W.

We were wandering around the Seattle Center, basking in a gloriously sunny Pacific Northwest day. The Seattle Center is the hub of Seattle, at least as far as points of interest are concerned. The famous Space Needle is there, along with several of the futuristic buildings built in 1962 for the World's Fair. Microsoft billionaire Paul Allen's amorphous and colorful stainless steel enshrouded rock 'n roll museum, aptly named the Experience Music Project, is also there. So in the space of a few city blocks you have some of the most unique architecture in the world. Naturally, you also have some of the most unique people in the world.

C. W. was standing quite still in front of a gift shop in the shadow of the Space Needle. He didn't have to move to attract attention, because he was a veritable collection of interesting signs, clothing, and artifacts. And buried beneath a snowy white beard, a straw hat, and a large pair of horn-rimmed glasses was the most pleasant facial expression you could ever see on one person.

The signs, printed on white paper plates, grabbed our attention first, because they all had spiritual significance. Several included the name of Jesus: "Jesus Loves You," "Jesus is Right On," and "Jesus is the Way." Another paper plate sign encouraged passers by: "May Your Joy Be Full, Amen." C. W. had a guitar strapped to his shoulder, and around his neck hung a harmonica. But he wasn't playing anything. He was just standing there in the sunshine, looking sweet—so sweet that we just had to talk to him.

C. W. sharing Jesus' love in the shadow of the Space Needle.

We introduced ourselves, asked his name, and just started talking about life and what he was doing. C. W. was retired on a pension, and he now found purpose and meaning in life by coming to the Seattle Center every day, rain or shine, to encourage people. After a while he sheepishly reached into his overalls and pulled out a plain cassette tape with a hand-printed label that said, "Songs by C. W." He offered to give it to us, and we were glad to accept. We wanted to pay for the tape, however, so we gave him the "suggested retail price" of $5.00.

As we got in our car later that day, we played C. W.'s cassette—a very homemade recording of some bluegrass-type music, most of which had a spiritual theme. We loved it. We talked about C. W. as we listened to his music, but rather than reflect on how much he was like the other interesting people we had seen in our travels, we commented on his uniqueness, and how much courage it took to be that unique. Given the same life circumstances, the rest of us would be too self-conscious or too fearful to be so different. We would lack the courage it takes to stand out in a crowd and stand up for what you believe.

It's hard to say how many lives C. W. touches there at the Seattle Center, but we can say this for sure: he touched ours. And all we can say is, "C. W., may you always have the courage to be yourself. God bless you."

*Make others
happy and the happiest
person will be you.*

KEEPING GOD
IN THE SMALL STUFF

OUR TRIP ACROSS AMERICA

BRUCE & STAN

G

uy Debbas is one happy guy. As one of the premiere chocolatiers in the world, he loves his profession. Rumor has it that Guy (his name rhymes with "key") consumes one and a half pounds of chocolate a day. When you ask him about it, he just smiles and says, "What I can tell you is that we ship out 10,000 pounds of chocolate a day."

The chocolate goes out in the form of custom candies (think Godiva, but much more gourmet), tantalizing truffles, and beautiful bars. De Bas Chocolate Company will cover almost anything in chocolate—coffee beans, raisins, cherries, and even wine (a De Bas specialty). They're all packaged with classy labels and shipped to specialty retailers like Dillards, as well as to countries all over the world.

*Courage is
standing still in
the strength of
the Lord.*

GUY DEBBAS

If you walked into Guy Debbas' chocolate factory like we did and literally smelled the success, you might think life has always been sweet for this jolly chocolatier. But you would be dead wrong. Behind the chocolate is a riveting story of faith and courage unlike any we heard on our trip across America.

Guy Debbas was born in Lebanon to a wealthy family known for its involvement in politics. His great uncle was Lebanon's first president when the country emerged as an independent state from France in 1943. Guy's father, who was Greek Orthodox, became a presidential candidate during the strife-torn early 1970s, when Christian Phalangists and Palestinian Muslims were on the verge of civil war. The family lived near Beirut in a 10,000 square foot home. Besides their political influence, they had varied business interests, including a chocolate factory.

In 1975 the Lebanese Civil War broke out, leading to a

sad chapter of violence that tore the country apart and destroyed its capital, once known as the jewel of the Mediterranean. Guy was a young idealist at the time who found comfort in religion. Like others in his family before him, he also took an interest in politics—so much so that he attracted the attention of the Phalangists, who threatened to kill him for taking a neutral stand during the war. Guy's father sent him to Egypt for safekeeping, but Guy couldn't stay away. Without alerting his family, the energetic Guy slipped back into Lebanon.

From that point forward events unfolded like a movie script, only this was very real. Guy's enemies—this time it was members of the Palestinian Communist Party—discovered his whereabouts and promptly kidnapped him. For more than a month he was kept bound and blindfolded, tortured and threatened with death if he didn't forsake his neutrality and persuade his father to do the same. Guy

So be strong and take courage, all you who put your hope in the Lord!

PSALM 31:24

refused. In an ironic twist, members of the Communist Party of Lebanon rescued him (he still doesn't know why), enabling him to rejoin his family.

But rather than find safety on the land his father had declared neutral, the Debbas family was singled out by the Socialist Party, which was in the middle of large-scale warfare. Guy said that in a two-day period, 6,000 people were killed and 30,000 left homeless. Then they burst into the Debbas home. Armed with machine guns and hollow-point, poisoned bullets, the terrorists lined up Guy's family and shot them all.

"They emptied a whole magazine on me and then shot

everyone else," Guy recalled. "Over 20 people perished, including my father, who died in my arms." Guy never lost consciousness during the horrific ordeal. He remembers very clearly crying out to God. "When I was lying there full of bullet holes, I made a clear decision to dedicate myself to Christ. I cried out in an audible voice, 'Jesus, help me.' I knew then and there that He would help me, and He did. Jesus helped me get to a hospital, He helped me live, and He helped me walk again when the doctors gave me no hope."

In fact, the doctors thought Guy was a corpse when he first arrived at the hospital more than two hours after the shooting. "He's dead," one doctor declared. "Why did you bring him to me? Take him to the morgue." Guy knew better. "No, I'm still here," he gasped.

"I don't know why God spared me and why other people suffer and die," Guy said. "I'm not special. But I know

Guy Delebras in his world-famous chocolate factory.

that God loves me,
and that He is
faithful to His
word."

After recovering from his
wounds, Guy came to California. Except for
three brothers, his entire family was gone, so there was
nothing to keep him in Lebanon. He met and married his
wife, Wendy, while attending college in Los Angeles, and
the two of them eventually moved to Fresno, where Guy
began importing chocolate from the factory he and his
brothers operated in Lebanon. As he became more and
more successful, his commitment to serve God took a

back seat to money and the desire for more wealth. That's when disaster struck Guy once again. At the same time Wendy and Guy's new home burned to the ground in Central California, terrorists leveled his factory in Beirut.

It would have been easy for Guy to give up, both on God and on his dream to build a successful chocolate business. But his wife reminded him that even though he had wavered in his commitment to God, there was no doubt that God was sticking to him.

"That was a huge turning point for me," Guy said. "Knowing that God will

Delicious
De Bas candies.

always love me and never be against me gave me great courage. I was running my life and my business as if they belonged to me, and when you take that position, it's easy to give up before you receive the blessing God promises. What I have learned—and this gives me great strength and courage every day of my life—is that you can never give up, no matter what the circumstances. You need to stand still and let the Lord take care of it."

For the past fifteen years Guy has "stood still" in the Lord as he has built De Bas Chocolatier into a successful company with an international reputation for excellence. Still, he takes nothing for granted. "Every day I remind myself to stand still in the strength of the Lord. He is my strength. He gives me courage."

Courage in the Flames

There's a lot of Montana between South Dakota and Idaho. We know it to be a fact because we drove across Montana. And it didn't happen quickly. But we didn't mind, because the scenery was beautiful. Wide-open spaces and dense forests were all we saw for hours and hours. But not all of Montana was so serene. At the very time we traveled through Montana, parts of it were ablaze with forest fires ravaging areas not too far from the Interstate.

The battle against the forest fires was the topic of conversation every place we stopped in Montana. (You can hardly manage to drive across the state without at least a one-night layover and multiple gas stops.) Stories of heroic firefighters were featured on the radio and television reports and in the newspaper. Among the many stories, one captured our attention. It was about Steve Moser, one of the 500 U. S. Army soldiers from Ft. Hood, Texas who had been flown in to help battle the inferno near Missoula, Montana.

Steve Moser carried a shovel just like all the other army soldiers on the fire line. But that's the closest thing to a weapon he has ever handled in his military career. Usually the only thing in his hands is a camouflage-covered Bible. Steve Moser is an army chaplain.

We wondered what an army chaplain was doing battling the wildfires in Montana. We knew that Moser might be able to preach a good sermon about fire and brimstone, but the safety of a pulpit seems far removed from fighting actual flames and dodging falling charred timbers. We had the initial impression of wimpy guy in a clerical collar cowering behind the *real* firefighters, all the while dosing himself with holy water. Then we found out

If you belong to God,

and other people know it,

they will be evaluating God

by what they see in you.

KEEPING GOD IN THE SMALL STUFF

more about Steve Moser and realized our initial impressions were all wet.

Instead of a clerical collar, Moser suited up like everyone else in battle fatigues, combat boots and a hard hat. He wielded his shovel side by side with the other soldiers as the ash and sparks swirled around them. This guy is no namby-pamby church boy. He was right there in the middle of the heat of the battle (pun intended), and he won the respect of his fellow soldiers and the seasoned professional firefighters.

"Even though I'm a chaplain, I still do the same work they do, and I do it right next to them," Moser reported about his relationship with the other guys on the fire line. "I do it because it builds bridges, and to me, that's big money. It builds rapport and credibility, and frankly, those are the bridges for the gospel. When those bridges are built, I can do ministry."

If you're wondering what king of "ministry" can take place on the burning, smoke-covered mountaintops of Montana, it's certainly not making quilts for the ladies missionary society. And it isn't all-night prayer meetings (although Moser prays with his buddies when it's appropriate). From what we could tell, Moser brings to the battle line exactly what the troops need: encouragement. Sometimes that encouragement is of a spiritual nature. Other times it may involve inquiring how a soldier's marriage is getting along. Whatever is bothering the guys, they know they can talk about it with Steve.

We've heard about religious fanatics who walk across burning coals in their bare feet. Then there's Steve Moser. He isn't a fanatic, but he has a genuine faith in God that gives him the courage to walk on burning ground. Only he wears combat boots when he does it.

Courage to Laugh at Yourself

One of the best things about driving across the country and meeting people is that the experience can change your preconceived notions and stereotypes. Take Iowans, for example. You probably think the residents of the sedate state of Iowa are down-to-earth, simple, somber people. You might even think they're a bit mundane, bordering on the edge of downright boring. That was certainly our impression and preconceived opinion. Of course, that was before we heard about the Farmall Promenade Tractor Square Dancers.

As we drove through the Midwest, we were confounded by reports of eight farmers who were touring the state of Iowa performing a square dance while driving their tractors.

Humor is
the shock absorber
of life; it helps us
take the blows.

—PEGGY NOONAN

These guys, ages forty-one to forty-nine, each drove a bright red, vintage Farmall tractor, as they ran through the paces of a precision driving team to square dance choreography. This was certainly not the stuffy, staid impression we originally had of Iowa farmers.

As it turns out, we *really* underestimated the fun-loving nature of these Iowa farmers. They apparently really get into the whole "do-cee-do" spirit and will perform only if it is done authentically. As every square-dance aficionado knows, half of the participants must be women. Unfortunately, there are no women in the ranks of the Farmall Promenade Tractor Square Dancers (which is further proof that women have a greater sense of self-dignity then men). So, four of the guys don curly wigs, inflatable bosoms, gingham blouses and denim skirts before they straddle their tractors.

If you're ever traveling through the Midwest and you

have a hankering to stop in Nehama, Iowa, then listen carefully for the sound of tractor engines. You wouldn't want to get plowed under by one of those farming "femme fatales" practicing their synchronized square-dancing maneuvers. Just to be on the safe side, get ready to run for cover if you hear a square-dance caller shouting the following cadence:

Four gents start, go all around,
Watch those tires churn up the ground!
Ladies spin out, circle to the right,
Gents go on, keep your tires tight!
Wheel meets wheel, hood meets hood,
Turn around, you're looking good!

Under the
arch in St. Louis
(that's Stan on
the right, but
it's not Bruce
on the left).

OUR TRIP ACROSS AMERICA

BRUCE & STAN

THE GATEWAY ARCH
IN ST. LOUIS

Quiet Courage

If courage were an animal it would be a lion, seemingly without fear.

If courage were a color it would be gray, like steel, full of strength.

If courage were a sound it would be silence.

Some people equate courage with a yell or a grunt forced through gritting teeth. The mental image is of a soldier charging into battle. But the noise may be nothing more than a mask for the fear the soldier feels. Other brave people stand up to opposition and their own fears with quiet dignity. It's hard to tell what they're feeling, or if they're even afraid. Often it's not until the battle is over that you realize how courageous they really were.

Courage is contagious.
When a brave man
takes a stand,
the spines of others are
often stiffened.

BILLY GRAHAM

Jackie is such a person. She is one of the most courageous people we've ever known; yet her courage is so quiet and filled with silent dignity that it probably passes right by most folks.

Jackie would be the first to tell you that what she is doing is no big deal, but we would strongly disagree. You see, even though Jackie isn't fighting for her life or the lives of others, she has quietly gone into battle for a principle she believes in. And that may be the toughest courage of all. When you're forced to react to a life-threatening circumstance, courage may be your only option. It certainly is the only way to overcome your fear. But when you're given the choice either to fight for a principle you believe in or to let it go, knowing that people will neither condemn nor commend you regardless of the outcome, then you know you're pretty much alone in your courage.

Such was the case when Jackie started teaching a Bible as Literature class in the high school where she's been a faculty member for nearly two decades. Never one to shrink from her faith in God, Jackie has always brought biblical principles into her classes, whether literature or history courses. While she has never crossed the line that separates "church and state" in the classroom, Jackie has always been available after class for any student who wanted to talk further about her faith. Jackie is equally passionate about helping struggling students with their class work. She often volunteers to tutor kids on Saturdays.

The Bible as Literature class, however, was a different assignment. First of all, the class was set up as a pilot program, which meant it would come under the watchful eye of community groups. Second, school and district officials decided to study the class and Jackie's way of teaching it after students had signed up and the semester had begun.

Jackie has devoted her life to students.

Sure enough, less than a month after the Bible as Literature class began, the administration at Jackie's school shut it down after receiving complaints from a local watchdog group. Outsiders expressed concern that the class was violating district policy, which prohibits teaching religion in the classroom. Jackie was stunned. Nothing like this had ever happened to her before. People leveled accusations at Jackie and tried to intimidate her into quitting. But she stood strong and steadfast in her own quiet way.

The greatest test of courage is to bear defeat without losing heart.

ROBERT G. INGERSOLL

Jackie's students had plenty to say about the closing of their class. More than a hundred students demonstrated at the high school in support of Jackie and the class. They chanted, "Save Bible Lit." Others carried signs that read, "It's Not About Religion." Reporters for the local paper were summoned to the scene, and they interviewed several students. "We're here to support our class, to save our teacher," one of them said. "We don't want to see her go. She's a great teacher. She has changed so many lives," said another.

The reporters looked for Jackie, but she was nowhere to be found. Jackie never said a word. In the days to come, when various ideas were proposed to reinstate the class—but without Jackie—she was silent. Even when she attended a public forum on the class, she didn't utter a word. Yet her presence and quiet resolve encouraged and strengthened everyone around her.

When the principal decided to reinstate the class with Jackie and a mentor teacher, she accepted the change, even though it was a disruption to her students and a slap in the face to someone with her experience and skill. She supported the plan and never said a word against it. In fact, it wasn't until Jackie sent a letter to the people who had sent her cards and letters of encouragement that she said anything at all, and still her words carried no bitterness whatsoever.

We received the letter, only a page in length, and it spoke volumes to us about the nature of courage. Jackie thanked everyone for their prayers and said they enabled her to get through the difficult times. True to Jackie's character, she blamed no one, but simply said she had learned a lot through the experience. Most of all, she expressed her love for Jesus and said she had come to realize how much people are offended by Him. It was a lesson for the ages.

As always, God is faithful. He was faithful to Jackie. Even though she wasn't battling in a physical life and death situation, she certainly stood her ground in the spiritual arena, where true courage is sometimes harder to find.

God doesn't often
give us huge opportunities that
are spectacular.
But He always gives us
small opportunities that
are significant.

KEEPING GOD IN THE SMALL STUFF

111

Courage to Care

It looks like any other house in the middle-class neighborhood. There's not even one distinguishing characteristic on the exterior. Hundreds, maybe thousands, of people drive by each day on the busy street that borders this house. None of them has any idea of the precious, invaluable treasures that lie within the modest home. But *we* knew—only because someone had told us the secret. And we were anxious to view what had been described to us as "priceless beyond measure."

While the exterior of the house is commonplace, a visitor gets a clue of something remarkable as soon as the front door is open. Throughout the house there are stuffed animals and the type of toys that would occupy an infant's attention. These items aren't confined to one room in the house that functions as a nursery. They are every corner of every room. But they are not strewn about in random fashion as if discarded by a torrent of toddlers running rampant through the house. No, there appears to be an orderly placement of the toys and stuffed animals. There appears to be a strategy or a system behind it all.

In striking contrast to the plethora of preschool paraphernalia, the house is also full of sophisticated medical equipment. There are monitors and breathing apparatus stationed near every couch. There are hospital beds and medical cribs in almost every room. The kitchen looks like the supply room for a pharmacy.

The house is known as the Allen-Spees Home. It is the realized dream of two women who have the courage to care for infants with special medical needs.

Others will see

our faith in action

before they see our faith

in heaven.

KEEPING GOD
IN THE SMALL STUFF

Friendships are often formed between two people who have something in common, and that's exactly how the friendship between Terry Spees and Sue Allen developed. But their common bond was not living in the same neighborhood or going to the same church or even car-pooling their kids to the same soccer team. Their common bond was the care of foster children.

H and Terry Spees have a house-full of kids. They always have. There have been fifteen kids living in the Spees home at one time or another over the past twenty years. While H and Terry will say that all of the kids are part of their family, no one would mistakenly believe they all share the same bloodline. Only three of the children are the biological offspring of H. and Terry. The others (four of whom have been adopted and the rest whom are staying with the Spees under foster care) represent a variety of nationalities. Because Terry is a nurse, many of the children they took into their home had special medical needs; some were prematurely born, some were drug exposed.

Mark and Sue Allen have also been foster parents for more than twenty years. They have opened their hearts and home to more than fifty children during that time. The first children invited into their home did not have medical challenges, but they came from backgrounds of neglect and abuse. Mark and Sue extended their love to these children in an effort to erase the emotional scars. After years of foster parenting, Mark and Sue also began to take on the responsibility of medically fragile infants.

Sue and Terry met each other through foster parenting.

They recognized in each other a shared love for special-needs infants. Terry and Sue believe that God orchestrated their shared ministry through their children. They both had severely disabled children in their care who required constant round-the-clock attention. The medical experts had predicted a short life expectancy for both children, but these two kids were survivors. As time passed, Terry and Sue both realized that the family setting made continual care almost impossible. They heard about a home in Oklahoma that provided care to four young children who were develop-

Each little life is precious.

mentally disabled and medically fragile. Upon hearing of that special place in Oklahoma, God gave Sue and Terry a shared vision to establish a care home in their town where developmentally disabled children could receive the best home life and quality care possible. But that's not all God gave them. He also gave them the courage to care for these children who are incapable of giving anything back in return.

There was more paperwork and bureaucracy required to obtain a license for their care home than Sue and Terry imagined. But they were undaunted. Finally, their license was issued and they opened the Allen-Spees Home in April of 1996. They each had a child in their foster care who moved into the house. There were four more spaces available, but the vacancies didn't last long. Within three months of opening, there was a waiting list. By July of 1997, Sue and Terry opened their second home, which was full immediately. At the time we met with them, they were in the process of preparing a third home.

The children in the residences of the Allen-Spees Home are so medically fragile that they would not have survived at birth had they been born ten years ago. But the recent advancements in medical technology have been able to sustain these precious lives. Some of these young children are on ventilator support or have tracheostomies; some are in a coma; one little boy is paralyzed and can't even blink. It takes courage and love to care for these children. Sue and Terry and the members of their staff have both of those character traits in large measure.

It is abundantly evident that Sue and Terry are not just working at a job. They are actively engaged in a caring ministry. We asked them how they combat discouragement when caring daily for these children in such tragic circumstances. They explained it as a matter of perspective. "I truly believe that God doesn't make mistakes," Terry

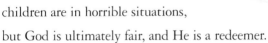

Every infant deserves to be loved.

told us. "He may have allowed this to happen, but He is still in control. These children are in horrible situations, but God is ultimately fair, and He is a redeemer. He has not forgotten or ignored these kids."

Terry went on to explain the role that she and Sue play in God's care for these kids: "My job is to figure out how I can best be God's hands and heart in this house. I'll assist Him in their daily care now, but He will handle redeeming these children unto Himself in the future. The Bible is full of verses that proclaim how much God cares for the

There is no child unloved by God.

---

disadvantaged. Those verses certainly include the kids in our homes. So, we take great comfort in the fact that we are ministering to children who are so special to God."

We don't mind admitting to you that we were moved to tears to see these kids and to hear Sue and Terry tell the stories behind each of those little lives. We assumed that everyone must have a similar response, but that isn't the case. Apparently there are people who view the circumstances of these lives and contend that a decision to terminate life should have been made before birth. We asked Sue and Terry how they respond to such comments. Here is their reply:

"A range of things can happen to you between the time

you're born to the day you die. If during that time your body and spirit remain in tact, then you are very fortunate. These little children are born with broken bodies, but their spirit is whole and in tact. They are potential full heirs to the throne of God. God has promised to meet all of our needs, and that promise applies to these kids. Because their bodies are so disabled, God must be communicating with them spiritually in a place and in a way that we may not even be aware of. These children are right in the middle of God's plan—more so than the rest of us—because they don't have the capacity to move out of it. For that reason, there is no need to pity them. God will have a special reward for them later. When we go to heaven, we are anxious to stand behind our kids and see what God is going to do for them."

After we said our thanks and good-byes to Sue and Terry, we returned to our rental car parked at the curb outside their house. We were back on the street where their house looks the same as all of the other ones on the block. But in our minds and heart we knew that it wasn't the same at all. The precious little guests in that home, and the courageous women who care for them, make it different. And we were different, too.

If you don't know how
to give comfort to others,
try to imagine yourself
in their place.

GOD IS IN THE SMALL STUFF

More Stories

We invite you to read some of the other stories
we heard in the course of our cross-country tour of America.
They have been collected in three additional books:

Stories We Heard About Joy
Stories We Heard About Love
Stories We Heard About Hope

And here are some other books we've written,
some of which are quoted in this one:

God Is in the Small Stuff
God Is in the Small Stuff For Your Family
Keeping God in the Small Stuff
Bruce & Stan's Guide to God
Bruce & Stan Search for the Meaning of Life

We'd love to hear from you. You can reach us by email at
guide@bruceandstan.com or through our Web site:
www.bruceandstan.com.